# Contents

# Introduction

## What is a minibeast?

Spiders, ants, ladybirds, woodlice, worms, snails and bees are just a few of the creatures that we call minibeasts.

## What is a minibeast hotel?

Most minibeasts will be very happy to occupy any place of shelter they come across and a child will readily conjure up and believe an imaginary world where minibeasts stay in hotels. So using the idea of a hotel – a place to stay which is comfortable for minbeasts to visit – is a brilliantly creative way to encourage children to explore and investigate the natural world. By providing a shelter or what is known as a 'minibeast hotel' children can have a first hand experience of seeing minibeasts in their natural habitat. From this kind of close observation they can begin to understand the needs and behaviour of minibeasts and perhaps change preconceived ideas of minibeasts being scary or dangerous.

In the real world, there are all kinds of designs of hotels from very basic to five star luxury and this can be the case with minibeast hotels too! People check into hotels for a night, a few days, or much longer and in a similar way this can be the same for minibeasts. Children can begin the process of considering for themselves questions such as:

▶ Who will stay in my minibeasts hotel and why?

▶ Will they stay long?

▶ What will they do when they stay?

Whenever possible, young children need to learn through first hand experiences about the world they live in. In their gardens, or on a walk, they will encounter living creatures and their natural curiosity means they will want to observe, touch, and ask many questions.

An average garden may be home to over 2,000 different species of insects. If your setting doesn't have a formal garden, you can enhance whatever outdoor area you do have by putting tubs of plants along an outside wall or attaching your minibeast hotel to an outside wall or fence. Brick walls

**Cumbria**
**County Council**

...ies, books ...d more . . .

Please return/renew this item by the last due date.
Library items may be renewed by phone on
030 33 33 1234 (24 hours) or via our website
**www.cumbria.gov.uk/libraries**

Cumbria Libraries
**CLIC**
Interactive Catalogue

Ask for a CLIC password

# The LITTLE book of Minibeast hotels

by Ann Roberts

Illustrations by Mike Phillips

**LITTLE BOOKS WITH BIG IDEAS**

Published 2011 by A&C Black, Bloomsbury Publishing plc
50 Bedford Square, London, WC1B 3DP
www.acblack.com

ISBN 978-1-4081-4049-9

Text © Ann Roberts
Illustrations © Mike Phillips, Beehive Illustration
Photograph on page 5 © Graham Flack

The author would like to thank Paul and Jill Longworth for their permission to allow
Harriet to be pictured on the front cover and on page 14, Peter Talbot for his support,
advice and his camera in the production of the photographs for this book and the staff
at Besses Children Centre for their willingness to test some of the ideas in this book.

Printed in Great Britain by Latimer Trend & Company Limited

This book is produced using paper that is made from wood grown in
managed, sustainable forests. It is natural, renewable and recyclable.
The logging and manufacturing processes conform to the environmental
regulations of the country of origin.

**To see our full range of titles
visit www.acblack.com**

and paving are places that insects move around on and if the area is slightly damp it will encourage them to stay!

Building a minibeast hotel provides learning experiences and encourages children to realise that some minibeasts help us and are part of the conservation of our planet. Once you've made your minibeast hotel, checking up on the occupants of the hotel is part of the fun and can be used to increase children's understanding that things change over time.

The Little Book of Minibeast Hotels is designed to encourage early years practitioners to enable, extend and develop children's interest in the outside natural world. Children love minibeasts and presenting activities around them sustains their interest in them.

This book will provide a wealth of ideas on how to construct a suitable 'hotel' according to the developmental stage that the children are at and the kind of environments that you have available. All the hotels featured in this book are cheap to make – most of the hotels are made from throwaway items that just need to be collected.

There is no limit to the hotels you can make and making a few may mean you can have several on the go at one time so that there is a higher chance of occupancy!

## Who or what might check into your minibeast hotel?

The hotels featured in this book have been designed to attract stag beetles, solitary bees, butterflies, spiders, lacewings and ladybirds.

## Resources – general information

None of the minibeast hotels featured are made with expensive items – they are often made from items that are surplus or that would be thrown away without thought. Recycling materials and using them for a purpose can encourage children to see resources in a much more creative light. This can also be an opportunity to raise children's awareness of being sensitive to the environment and using waste in a positive and effective way.

The very simplest design involves a newspaper and a bottle – everyday resources which can be used by parents at home, in a childminding environment or brought into an early years setting by children or supplied by practitioners. This also allows children to make the habitats as individuals or as part of a group activity and then cascade the idea into their own garden environment. A full resource list is provided on pages 44-45.

## Health and safety

The construction of the minibeast hotels can vary from a simple collection of bamboo canes tied together to a more complex 'high rise model'. Young children will benefit from using different materials and, to some extent, from having some risks in their play.

An adult presence and possible intervention is there to ensure the safety of all children at all times and comply with welfare regulations. It is important to allow children to attempt some of the constructions themselves, sensitively intervening and promoting independence but not letting children feel frustrated if they can't do it.

Here are some things that you need to consider:

▶ Make sure that tools and resources are appropriate for the age and developmental stage of the children – consider what skills and knowledge they are building on and what extensions of their experiences are needed.

▶ Ensure that children lift and carry items in a safe way for themselves and others close to them.

▶ When pushing items into holes and gaps remind the children to take care so that injuries to themselves, or others nearby can be avoided.

▶ Children exploring and touching items outside must wash their hands when they go back inside and wear appropriate clothes (especially footwear) when outside.

## Benefits

Spending time outdoors is an essential aspect of a healthy lifestyle. Observing who or what comes and visits the hotel over periods of time, encourages a sustained interest in the world outside. If there is an unusual find then it will promote questioning, research and further observation. These activities extend learning and challenge children's thinking.

If children are involved in making the hotels and choosing the locations they will have a sense of ownership of the whole activity and it is more likely to sustain their interest and enjoyment.

Teaching young children not to be afraid of minibeasts is another positive outcome of this kind of work. Making minibeast hotels presents an opportunity to support and encourage children to handle the materials used for the hotel construction and to closely observe living creatures.

## Links with EYFS Curriculum (from the draft version 2011)

All the activities in this book can be linked to:

### The prime areas of the EYFS

**Personal, Social and Emotional Development**
Children are encouraged to talk about ideas, express their own opinions, choose resources and state when they need help. Making relationships is part of this prime area, as is working cooperatively in a group, taking turns and helping each other – all of which are key skills for children constructing minibeast hotels.

**Physical Development**
Children will experience handling various tools and equipment as they construct the minibeast hotels independently and in groups. Given the nature of using natural materials and being outside, children will learn about hygiene and safety issues too.

**Communication and Language**
Speaking, listening and expressing their thoughts will arise because of the nature of the very practical work and time in the outside environment. As children watch to see the outcomes of their projects, e.g. who comes to visit their minibeast hotel, they will be required to give opinions and construct questions and answers.

# The specific areas of learning and development

## Literacy

Many literacy links are provided: songs and rhymes related to minibeasts (pages 51-54) and useful lists of books and websites (pages 54-56) to find out more about minibeasts and insect hotels. Children enjoy hearing and sharing stories about small creatures and saying rhymes and chants for themselves and to others. Early writing and drawing are also encouraged.

## Mathematics

There are many counting opportunities, e.g. counting how many minibeast visitors there are to an hotel or counting how many items fill up a space in the different sections of the hotels. The numerous containers (and spaces created between them in the minibeast hotels) provide ample opportunities to talk about and handle shapes.

## Understanding the world

Children learn about similarities and differences in relation to objects, materials and living things in the natural world. Children make observations about animals and learn about change and the life cycle of living things.

## Expressive arts and design

Children explore textures, design, shape and form. There are opportunities for children to use minibeasts in song and dance in imaginative ways, e.g. children can sing and mimic the movement of animals. The use of photography, drawing and creating displays are all encouraged and linked to the activities.

# Roll-up hotel

## What you need:

- ▶ plastic bottles (soft drinks bottles of small, medium and large size)
- ▶ an old newspaper (ideally broadsheet size)
- ▶ a pair of scissors
- ▶ insect friendly glue – made from flour and water
- ▶ string

## What and why:

This activity encourages young children to use their hand-eye skills and fine motor skills to construct tubes made from newspaper and then explore the shape and space of a bottle.

## Before you start:

Ensure that the bottles are clean and dry inside. Allow the children to look through, compare, roll and feel the shape of a variety of different plastic bottles. Encourage the children to make a bottle collection and sort it into groups.

## What you do:

1. Cut the plastic bottle in half and discard the top half.

2. Open out the newspaper. You will need to have at least three sheets to fill the bottle.

3. If necessary cut the newspaper to the length of the bottle.

4. Help the children to take one of the lengths of newspaper and roll it into a tube about the size of the bottle top or slightly smaller – just big enough to make a tunnel for the minibeasts to crawl down.

5. To seal the tube shape and prevent it from unrolling, use special insect friendly glue – made from flour and water. If children find it difficult to hold the rolled tube whilst gluing it,help them to roll it around a pencil or another similar-sized cylinder to make it easier to grip.

6. When they have rolled and glued several sheets, pack them into the bottle – make sure they are tight and can't fall out.

7. Help the children to tie a large piece of string around the bottle. Hang it up in the garden and await the arrival of your first hotel guests!

## And another idea:

▶ Use smaller sized bottles to make a minibeast 'mini hotel'.
▶ Children can take photographs of the project to record their learning journey.

# Lacewing hotel

## What you need:

- a plastic bottle (a medium/large size soft drinks bottle)
- corrugated cardboard or bamboo tubes (available from garden centres)
- a pair of scissors
- string

## What and why:

This activity encourages young children to use their hand-eye skills and dexterity. Ideally this activity would be better for the later end of the Early Years Foundation Stage when children are more able generally and have more experience of using scissors and other sharp implements.

## Before you start:

Lacewings are common in the garden but many children might not have heard of or seen them before – gather some pictures of lacewings from books and the internet and show them to the children.

Ensure that the bottle is clean and dry inside.

## What you do:

1. Carefully cut about 10 centimetres off the bottom of the plastic drinks bottle.

2. Help the children to make a hole in the bottle lid.

3. Take some string, and show the children how to thread it though the bottle lid and tie a knot on the inside of the lid.

4. Now take the corrugated card and roll it carefully, then squash it into the bottle so nothing hangs out. Alternatively push in cut-to-size bamboo tubes.

5. Screw the bottle lid back on.

6. Tie the bottle (the minibeast hotel) to a hanging branch of a tree or a hedge.

## And another idea:

▶ Using tissue paper and wire make some lacewing models. Children will have to be gentle with the tissue paper as they hold it – remind them that insects need delicate handling too and can easily be harmed by humans.

# Buzzing around bee hotel

## What you need:

- pipe or tube made of wood
- small bamboo canes that will fit inside the pipe
- rough garden string

## What and why:

There are many different species of bee that will nest in tunnels and tubes. The female of the non-aggressive mason bee species spends most of her life searching for hollow stems to use as a nest. So why not make a bee hotel for her where she can lay her eggs?

In recent years there has been a rapid decline in bees and preserving them in the environment is very important.

## Before you start:

Some children may be afraid of bees because of having been stung in the past. Talk about the need to be careful when in close proximity to bees and other stinging insects. Talk about the positive impact that bees have and the role they play in honey making.

## What you do:

1. Show the children the tube or pipe that is the outer part of the hotel. Wrap the string around the outer cylinder and make loops of string on each side – like long handles – these are so you can hang the cylinder in the trees or shrubbery.

2. Help the children to insert into the tube or pipe the bamboo canes which need to fit in neatly and tightly so they don't fall out. Fill the cylinder up fully.

3. Hold the bee hotel up and make sure the string is even so that you can hang it in the site you have chosen.

## And another idea:

▶ Same hotel – different design: Carefully pack a rectangular wooden frame with straight hollow stems such as reeds, bamboo canes or old flower stems. Only as you add the final few does the whole lattice lock solid. Hang your bee hotel from a hook on a sunny wall.

# Flowerpot hotel

## What you need:

▶ a large plastic or terracotta flowerpot

▶ bamboo tubes used for lawn edging (available from your local garden centre)

▶ smooth wire

## What and why:

Using a flowerpot to make a minibeast hotel is ideal for younger children as they can construct this independently with little or no help and see an instant result. Leaving the flowerpot on its side makes it easily accessed and viewed at the children's level.

## Before you start:

Discuss with the children where this hotel could be sited and talk about who might visit the minibeast hotel. If there is an old empty flowerpot lying around your setting's garden, have a look inside and see if there are already any insects around or near the empty flowerpot.

## What you do:

1. Decide on a position where the flowerpot will be set at ground level, and place it on its side. Make sure you bed it into the ground so that it doesn't roll around or move.

2. Show the children the bamboo tubes, which should be bound together with wire. Let the children roll the bundle of smooth bound tubes around on the ground, exploring the shape and texture of the materials. Make sure there are no sharp pieces of wire sticking out which could cut the children's hands.

3. Put the bamboo tubes into the flowerpot and gently loosen them so that they touch the edges of the flowerpot.

## And another idea:

▶ Fill a small terracotta flowerpot with as much straw as possible. Turn the flowerpot upside down and stick it on top of a wooden cane or pole so it won't fall off. Then put this ideal ladybird or lacewing shelter in a quiet area of the garden.

# Ferret towers hotel

## What you need:

▶ two ferret tunnels (available from pet shops or the pet supply section in your local garden centre)

▶ straw

▶ bamboo, cane or straws

## What and why:

Ferret tunnels are made of willow – they are cylinders of willow with small window sections in them. These are rarely available in the normal equipment within an early years setting and therefore children will have a first experience of seeing and using them.

## Before you start:

Let the children explore the ferret tunnels – feeling the willow and putting their hands in and out of the windows of the tunnels.

Talk about how the natural brown colour of the tunnel matches the surrounding environment, especially in the autumn and winter months. Talk about camouflage and explain what the tunnels are used for and remember some children may not have heard of or seen a ferret before and this may lead to a new learning experience.

## What you do:

1. Decide where you want to have the tunnels. Place one down on the ground and one standing up. Make sure that they are secure and in a sheltered place, otherwise they could fall down or get pushed over.

2. Push the bamboo or straws in the window section of the tunnels – ensure they are packed tightly so that they are secure.

3. Collect dried/dead leaves or cuttings from around the garden.

4. Surround the tunnels with the dead leaves and any other vegetation to camouflage the hotel into the environment.

## And another idea:

▶ Join two tunnels together (one on top of each other) to create a 'high rise' minibeast hotel.

▶ Using natural garden string, secure the bottom tunnel into the earth and then push hessian cloth, straws or bamboo sticks into the window spaces.

# Juice carton hotel

## What you need:

▶ an empty juice or milk carton or wine box

▶ old tubes

▶ bamboo cane

▶ straws

▶ corrugated card

▶ scissors

▶ string

## What and why:

Recycling items and putting them to good use teaches children about how items can be reused and how this helps to save the planet.

Thinking about using items creatively also gets children to use their imagination.

## Before you start:

Ask the children to draw pictures of things they could make with recycled boxes or cartons. Clean the boxes out and ensure they are dry and ready to work with. Gather together the other resources.

## What you do:

1. Cut out a window on one side of the box leaving a 4cm or 5cm edge round it.

2. Then make two holes in the top of the box. Feed some string through the holes to create a handle or 'hanging string'.

3. Help the children to roll the bamboo, straws or corrugated card into small bundles.

4. Show the children how to push the bamboo, straws, corrugated card through the window.

5. Hang the box up under a tree or on a bush.

## And another idea:

▶ Use an inexpensive wine rack as a framework for a minibeast hotel. In each hole where a wine bottle would fit push in corrugated card, bamboo sticks, sacking and straw. Children could combine different materials that they have used in previous, more basic hotels.

# Brick hotel

## What you need:

- gardening gloves
- house bricks (the kind with holes in them)
- a container to place the bricks in, for example:
  - ▷ a hessian cloth shopping bag
  - ▷ an old wooden box
- dry leaves, straw and twigs

## What and why:

You will find all kinds of minibeasts under stones, old slates and bricks in the garden, commonly woodlice and worms. These are ideal items to make an insect hotel.

## Before you start:

Spend some time looking for discarded bricks. Wearing protective gardening gloves, very carefully and slowly lift them up and look to see if there are some interesting minibeasts around, in or under them. If the bricks have moss or other growths on them leave this on!

## What you do:

1. Explain clearly how it's important to hold heavy items carefully and grip them well, and how it's important to protect your hands with gloves.

2. Group the bricks together in the container and then surround the hotel with dry leaves, straw and twigs that the children have collected.

3. Ensure that the bricks are safely secured and then keep a watch on them to see if anything comes to visit!

## And another idea:

▶ Use wooden pallets to strengthen and sandwich bricks – this enables the bricks to be built up higher. Layering the pallets and adding in various items such as pipes, straw or old flowerpots creates a 'high rise' minibeast hotel.

# Wire basket motel

## What you need:

▶ a half wire wall basket (from your local garden centre or pound shop)

▶ a roll of bamboo edging

▶ straw and bracken or leaves

▶ hessian cloth

I will need

## What and why:

The semi-circular shape of this minibeast hotel offers different possibilities for the different materials that can be fitted inside. Allowing children to see different shapes in the environment and recognise them out of context shows they can apply mathematical knowledge.

## Before you start:

Show the children the half wire basket and let them explore it and experiment with putting different shaped items inside it. By experimenting they will discover what is too big or what shapes can and can't fit or how many of the same item can fit into the space.

## What you do:

1. Position the half wire basket in a bush or place it with the flat part against a wall.

2. Show the children the roll of bamboo edging – this is medium sized bamboo canes attached together in a row that can be used to line the inside of the wire basket. Insert the roll of bamboo edging into the basket.

3. Help the children to push the hessian cloth, straw, bracken and leaves into the gaps.

## And another idea:

▶ You could make your hotel from a full circular wire planter. This is best attached by its bottom to a wall, allowing items to be packed easily into it. You could fill the planter with recyclable items that the children have collected.

# Hanging basket hotel

## What you need:

▶ an old hanging basket

▶ small pipes (house)

▶ straw, bracken, old leaves, dried up foliage

▶ string

## What and why:

Why not use an old hanging basket as a basis for a minibeast hotel? A simple plastic hanging basket will suffice. The position of the hanging basket will have already been established and this is just a case of changing its usage.

## Before you start:

Take the hanging basket down from where it has been hanging and gather all the items you want to use to make the minibeast hotel. Empty the hanging basket – you might find some minibeasts living there already!

## What you do:

1. Tie four or five pipes together and put them in the hanging basket.

2. Help the children to stuff each of the pipes with straw and bracken and old leaves. These materials present the minibeasts with different options as you will discover that some insects prefer one size or type of material to another.

3. Check that the pipes are safely secured in the basket – attach them with string if you are in any doubt.

4. Hang up the minibeast hotel – then wait and watch!

## And another idea:

▶ Group different sized cylinders into bunches and tie them together with string. Then hang them from trees or bushes like mobiles.

# Tin can hotel

## What you need:

▶ empty food tins or a large catering can or old oil drum

▶ old pipes

▶ small flowerpots

▶ canes

▶ hessian/straw

## What and why:

'Recycle, Renew, Repair' is an important message for young children to learn and encourages them to think about caring for the environment.

Using larger containers such as a catering can means that a small group of children can work as a group and construct the minibeast hotel together pooling as many ideas as possible and working collaboratively.

## Before you start:

Always check, well before any child comes into contact with the old containers, that they are safe to touch. Ensure that there are no rough edges or any remnants of dangerous substances inside the containers.

Gather all the resources and put them outside ready for a small group of children to explore. Let the children look at the containers and discuss with them what they could be used for rather than just being thrown away.

## What you do:

1. Once a large container has been identified, whether it is a metal tin can or a large box, let the children look into it and see the size of it.

2. Let the children explore and investigate the resources. Allow them plenty of time to touch and talk about the different items.

3. Help the children to fill the empty container with the various materials you have collected. Grouping items together is useful as then they will fit together well in the space and any gaps can be identified. Plug the gaps with straw and bracken.

4. Position the container under a bush, or another sheltered place in the garden, and then visit it regularly to see if you have any guests staying at your minibeast hotel.

## And another idea:

▶ Provide children with very open-ended resources such as empty tins and boxes for them to use as construction resources. Providing a large collection of empty containers encourages children to explore shape and space and use their vivid imaginations!

# Barrel and bamboo edging hotel

## What you need:

▶ an old garden planting barrel

▶ a roll of bamboo edging

## What and why:

Recycled old containers from the garden are brilliant for minibeast hotels! If there are small gaps or cavities in the sides so much the better as insects will love to crawl into these holes.

## Before you start:

Ensure your recycled container is safe for use. Check for any rough edges or splinters before showing the children the container. Brush it down with a hard kitchen brush to get rid of any unwanted debris.

## What you do:

1. Let the children explore the barrel – looking inside it and rolling it around the ground. Talk about they way the sides curve – it's a little like a cave when it is sat on its side.

2. Help the children to roll up the bamboo edging, giving them time to practise and repeat several times. Talk about the shape again – does it look a bit like a snail's shell? The use of the word 'spiral' may be appropriate for older children.

3. Insert the rolled up bamboo edging into the barrel and allow it to loosen up and fill the space up.

4. Now observe and see who visits this hotel – remember it won't happen immediately!

## And another idea:

▶ Using smaller containers lets each child be the owner of their own hotel. Allow each child to choose from a range of resources so that the minibeast hotels are unique and represent an individual approach from each child. See who gets visitors first!

# Plug planter hotel

## What you need:

▶ plastic plug seedling trays (available from your local garden centre)

▶ a wooden box or small table

▶ old leaves and other small pieces of foliage

▶ scissors

## What and why:

Very young children's concentration span and fine motor skills are still developing. This minibeast hotel can be built quickly and allows the younger end of the early years foundation stage to construct a hotel and see the result almost immediately.

## Before you start:

Investigate the plug seedling trays. Let children put leaves, and other small items they have found outside, in them.

## What you do:

1. Show the children the outside shape (the box or table) of the minibeast hotel.

2. Experiment putting the correct amount of seedling trays into the space.

3. If necessary, cut the seedling trays to fit the space.

4. Ensuring that the trays are secure, let the children place leaves and straw inside the compartments.

## And another idea:

▶ Collect bricks or flowerpots and push them into a pile of straw or bracken or piles of old leaves.

▶ Collect empty plastic bottles and bind them together using masking tape.

# Robin box hotel

## What you need:

▶ a small bird box (recycled or bought from your local garden centre, hardware store or pound shop)

▶ old newspapers

▶ scissors

## What and why:

As this minibeast hotel is bought ready-made this is a good activity if you want to focus on observation. Watching and looking very carefully to see what changes happen in the bird box means that children need to visit the hotel regularly and see what has happened.

## Before you start:

When you show the bird box to the children, first present it as a just a wooden box – the actual shape – rather than a 'bird box'. Look at the shape, size and how it is made. Then ask the children to guess what they think it might be used for. You could look at some photos of bird boxes in a book or on the internet. To avoid confusion, explain how you are going to reuse or recycle this bird box to make a minibeast hotel.

## What you do:

1. Help the children to cut and then roll up old newspaper into rolls roughly the length and width of pencils and gather a handful together. Alternatively, you can use shortened bamboo tubes (similar to those used to support garden plants).

2. Push the rolls of newspaper (or bamboo tubes) into the empty gaps at the top of the bird box. Make sure that they are tightly packed in.

3. Decide together where you will place the bird box – ideally in a shady spot or place you have spotted minibeasts visit before, such as a damp or mossy corner.

### And another idea:

▶ Fill an empty (deep) biscuit tin with tubes of corrugated card. Position it amongst long grass or other foliage.

# Tub hotel

## What you need:

- ▶ circular food containers and tubs
- ▶ sacking, twigs and straw
- ▶ markers and sticky lables
- ▶ strong PVA glue or sticky tape
- ▶ scissors
- ▶ small spades and bug catchers

## What and why:

Recycling old containers supports the idea of 'eco schools and settings'. Encourage children to have a positive attitude towards recycling, and use critical thinking and imagination to suggest how everyday things could be reused for different purposes.

## Before you start:

Set up a 'kid friendly' arts and crafts area in your setting. Collect and display all the items you need to make the tub hotel. Talk about the various food containers and tubs that you have collected – their shapes, what they are made of and what they could be reused for that would be environmentally friendly.

## What you do:

1. Let the children choose three or four containers and place them together to make a group of containers. Look how they fit together – where are there gaps?

2. Take the three or four tubs and using sticky tape or strong PVA glue, join them together (similar to a junk modeling activity).

3. Let the children decorate the tubs and put their names on the outside of the containers, using the sticky labels and markers.

4. With the children's input, write some minibeast hotel rules on another sticky label and glue it to the container. The rules might include:

   ▶ Please approach this hotel quietly so as not to scare the guests away!

   ▶ Please look carefully and do not disturb the guests in their rooms

   ▶ Photos are allowed

5. Ask the children to line the inside of the containers with the sacking, straw and twigs. Use the scissors to trim any excess material that is poking out.

6. Then, fill the hotel with fresh leaves, grass and a container of water – a plastic bottle cap is ideal.

7. Go on a bug hunt around the garden – collecting any possible occupants for the hotel, e.g. ants, beetles, worms. Use spades or bug jars to catch them if children are squeamish about using their bare hands. Remind the children to be gentle with any minibeasts that they collect. Ensure that the children wash their hands after touching any minibeasts.

## Tips and warnings:

▶ The sticky tape should ensure that, whatever the weather, the tubs with be joined - check regularly that they are still joined together.

▶ Ensure the position of your hotel is sheltered and embedded in earth as the tubs and their contents are light and could blow away.

▶ Beware of birds moving items around or stealing the contents of your hotel for their nests!

▶ Take notice of what the bugs are eating and add more of those plants to the 'hotel'.

# Ladybird high rise hotel

## What you need:

- a thin log measuring about 30cms long
- three pieces of squared wood (two to make the roof) and one to make the floor
- a pole
- wood glue
- small nails and hammer
- a hand drill (safety goggles and protective gloves)

## What and why:

Children might see insects in books, and on television but seeing something in its natural habitiat is another thing. The realisation of how small and delicate a minibeast can be, and how harmless it is an important part of learning about living things.

## Before you start:

Ensure there is sufficient space for using wood and tools and all health and saftey regulations are adhered to. When you are drilling the wood make sure the children stay at a safe distance.

## What you do:

1. Carefully drill holes in the thin log about 10cms apart. Ensure that the log is secured so there is no opportunity for slippage or accidents.

2. Take the two roof pieces and place then at right angles – to create the shape of a roof. Use strong glue (or small tacks) to attach the two pieces of wood together. If you have used glue, leave to dry.

3. Secure the roof on to the log using small tacks or glue.

4. Attach the other squared piece of wood on the bottom of the minibeast hotel – to act as a floor/base.

5. Glue the log onto the bottom of the minibeast hotel.

6. Place the high rise hotel into lawns, sheltered flower beds, wooded glades or even in planters. Make sure your tower is in a sheltered, warm spot of your garden.

## And another idea:

▶ If providing suitable tools is an issue for your setting, there are similar commercially produced minibeast hotels to be found in good garden centres or on the internet.

# Pipe and straws hotel

## What you need:

▶ a clay or plastic pipe

▶ drinking straws

▶ sticking tape or string

▶ scissors

I will need

## What and why:

This is one of the simplest of the minibeast hotels so is ideal for very
young children who can make a minibeast hotel by themselves. The
design is a low budget and quickly achieved construction.

## Before you start:

If there are groups of children making these hotels check that you have enough resources (drinking straws) available.

## What you do:

1. Children cluster as many straws together as it's possible to grip in their hands. Then help them to wrap sticky tape around the straws to make a secure bundle.

2. Children insert the bundle of straws into the pipe and continue to make several more bundles, each time inserting them into the pipe until it is completely filled.

3. Position the pipe in the garden area, ideally amongst rough grass. The children should surround the pipe with straw.

4. Observe and see what visitors come to stay!

## And another idea:

▶ Collect other 'pipe-like' materials and straw. Insert the materials into a house or plumber's pipe and where there are any gaps stuff with straw.

# Circular minibeast hotel

## What you need:

- chicken wire or plastic mesh (1m²)
- garden string, wire or twine
- a flat piece of wood or plastic
- pile of dead leaves, sticks, twigs and dead plant stems
- protective gardening gloves

## What and why:

Understanding that minibeasts have a place of their own to live and observing them in their environment develops knowledge and understanding of the world outside the children's own environment.

## Before you start:

Ensure you have conducted the appropriate risk assessment for this activity and provided children with protective gloves as they will be handling sharp chicken wire.

## What you do:

1. Roll the chicken wire or plastic mesh to make a tube. Tie the string, wire or twine around the tube to hold it securely.

2. Carefully show the children how to feed the sticks, dead plant stems or twigs through the holes near the bottom of the tube. The twigs overlap to form a mesh which will stop the leaves falling out of the bottom even if you pick the tube up; it also stops the leaves touching the ground and helps to stop them from getting damp.

3. Let the children fill the tube with the dead leaves.

4. Now give your hotel a roof. Do this by putting a piece of old wood or hardboard on top to stop the rain getting in. Alternatively, you could use an old bit of plastic with rocks placed on top to stop it blowing away!

5. In time, the leaves will bed down and so you will need to keep topping up with more – ask the children to check this regularly and add more leaves when necessary.

6. Place the hotel in a quiet shady part of the garden.

## And another idea:

▶ Your hotel does not have to be circular. Why not mould the chicken wire into other shapes? Consider using a pyramid shape or a square shape.

# Top tips on siting minibeast hotels

It is very important that the minibeast hotels are sited in sheltered places, out of areas which might catch strong winds and ideally close to vegetation.

Some of the minibeast hotels are suitable for hanging from trees, bushes, arches or pergolas, whereas some designs are better hung on a fence or wall.

If you have an area where you plan to site the minibeast hotel and you are aware that aphids are a problem (you have spotted them on plants) then siting the minibeast hotels close by is a positive indicator that this is an area that minibeasts frequent. Similarly, damp areas attract minibeasts.

# General resource list

- ▶ bird boxes
- ▶ bricks and concrete blocks (preferably with holes)
- ▶ cardboard tubes and corrugated cardboard
- ▶ chicken wire or plastic mesh
- ▶ crushed brick and concrete rubble
- ▶ deadwood – twigs, sticks and logs of all sizes up to half a metre long
- ▶ drinking straws
- ▶ dry leaves
- ▶ empty food containers (cartons, boxes and tins)
- ▶ ferret tunnels
- ▶ hessian cloth or sacking
- ▶ hollow bamboo canes of various sizes
- ▶ logs (drilled with various sized holes)
- ▶ newspapers
- ▶ pallets or strips of wood
- ▶ planting barrels or other wooden boxes

- plastic bottles
- plastic and clay pipes of various sizes
- plastic plug seedling trays
- plastic or terracotta flowerpots
- roofing felt
- roof tiles
- rough garden string
- sand
- stones
- straw or hay
- wire wall and hanging baskets

# Minibeast glossary

### Ants

There are thousands of different species of ants in the world. Ants can range in size from 2-25mm long. An ant has a large head, two antennae, a slender oval abdomen joined to its midsection by a small waist. It has two sets of jaws: the outer pair is used for carrying food and digging, and the inner pair is for chewing. Ants live in colonies and have a highly intelligent caste (or class) system within the colony – queens, males and workers. The ants you see in your garden will be black garden worker ants who will be very busy collecting food and building their nest. An ant's nest will be typically under the ground, or under a rock and will be made from twigs and gravel. The queen ant lives in the colony laying eggs. Ants eat aphids, small insects, seeds and nectar. The social behaviour of ants (along with bees) is the most complex in the insect world.

## Bees

Bees are flying insects closely related to wasps and ants, and are known for their role in pollination and for producing honey and beeswax. Bees feed on sweet nectar and pollen from flowers. There are many different species of bee but the best-known is the honeybee species which, as its name suggest, produces honey. Bees live in a beehive. A beehive is made up of a densely-packed matrix of hexagonal cells made of beeswax, called a honeycomb. Bees have a sting in their tail. Although a bee sting can be deadly to those with allergies, virtually all bees are non-aggressive if undisturbed and many can't sting at all. In people who are allergic to bee stings, a sting may trigger a dangerous anaphylactic reaction that is potentially fatal. A honeybee which is away from the hive, foraging for nectar or pollen will rarely sting, except when stepped on or treated roughly.

## Beetles

There are more than 800,000 species of insect on earth, more than all the other plant and animal species combined. Of this great number of insects, nearly half are beetles. Unlike other insects, beetles have a pair of leathery protective wings called elytra that cover their membranous flight wings. During flight, the elytra are spread apart and the two flight wings are unfolded and extended. Beetles come in a variety of shapes and colours, from red 'ladybirds' and metallic green fig beetles to lightning beetles that glow in the dark and huge horned beetles resembling a miniature rhinoceros! Beetles range in size from less than a millimetre to tropical giants of over six inches long.

## Caterpillars

Caterpillars have distinct heads and are segmented and wormlike. They have three pairs of short, legs jointed on the thorax. In addition, they have unjointed, fleshy appendages, called prolegs, on some abdominal segments. There is a row of simple eyes on either side of the body. Almost all caterpillars are vegetarian and have strong jaws for chewing. The chewing mouth parts and the prolegs disappear during the pupa stage, as the larva is transformed into an adult. Caterpillars have silk glands that open into a mouth part called the spinneret. The caterpillar exudes a silk strand continuously as it moves along; small caterpillars swing by the strand when dropping from a height. Many caterpillars use the thread to build a cocoon in which to pupate. Most molt their skin (to accommodate growth) five or six times before pupation. Some caterpillars have smooth skin; others are hairy, such as the woolly bear. Caterpillars form the major part of the diet of many birds and other animals. Caterpillars are voracious eaters and some cause considerable damage.

## Earthworms

Britain has about 16 species of earthworm likely to be found in gardens. They vary in size and colour, but all have a role to play in creating good soil structure and fertility. Earthworms eat decaying plant material and do not damage growing plants. Some earthworms emerge at night to feed on the surface, and will pull fallen leaves and other plant debris into their tunnels. Earthworms can be active throughout the year but are inactive during cold or hot and dry weather. They occur in most soils, but are scarce in soils that are extremely acidic or prone to waterlogging.

## Lacewings

Lacewing adults are slender-bodied flies with two pairs of wings covered with a network of veins – hence the name Lacewing. They are often green in colour and have long antennae. Both adults and larvae feed voraciously on greenfly and other aphids so they are valuable to gardeners. These insects hibernate as adults, and will readily come into houses in autumn. Their appearance changes in winter as their bodies turn pale pink. They are approximately 2-3 centimetres long. They are mainly seen from April to October. Their common habitats are parks, gardens and meadows.

## Ladybirds

Ladybirds are not only attractive, they are also very useful to gardeners and farmers because their diet is made up almost entirely of plant lice – small soft-bodied insects that invade garden plants and crops. Ladybirds eat plant lice both as adults and larvae. A sole ladybird eats thousands of plant lice during its lifetime, but also other plant-destroying insects. Some ladybirds also eat the fungi which attacks plants. Most ladybirds do not live more than one year. The adults hibernate in sheltered dry places or under leaves in warmer places.

## Spiders

Spiders are invertebrates – they don't have backbones. Spiders are not insects. An insect has three body parts and six legs. Spiders have eight legs and two body parts – the abdomen and the thorax. Most spiders have either six or eight eyes! Spiders are very useful little creatures – they help plants reproduce by pollinating them, help recycle dead trees and animals back into the earth, and are also a vital source of food for birds, fish and small mammals. There are more than 30,000 species of spiders in the world. Not all spiders spin webs. The ones that do spin webs have silk spinning glands called spinnerets at the tip of their abdomen.

## Wasps

Wasp is the common name applied to most species of hymenopteran insects, except bees and ants. Insects known as wasps include sawflies, the parasitic wasps, and the stinging wasps, which are the best known. About 75,000 species of wasp are known, most of them parasitic. Wasps are characterized by two pairs of membranous wings and an ovipositor (tube for laying eggs) that may be modified in various ways. In some species, one sex may be wingless. The larvae of parasitic wasps consume the bodies of other insects or, in a few cases, consume plant tissue. Most stinging wasps are predators or scavengers; their ovipositors may be modified to inject venom used for killing prey or for defence.

All female stinging wasps can defend themselves and their nests by using their ovipositor to inject venom. Males do not have a stinger. Most people can survive many stings, responding with only temporary pain and swelling, but for hyperallergic individuals (about 1% of the population) a wasp sting can be fatal.

## Woodlice

Woodlice are also known as sow-bugs or slaters. There are over 4000 species of woodlice (isopods) in the world. There are 37 species of British and Irish woodlice but there are a few introduced species which can breed indoors only. Most range in size from 5-15 mm. Most are grey or grey/brown and active mainly during the night. UK woodlice (and most others) feed mainly on rotting vegetation, and so help to return valuable nutrients to the soil. Woodlice rarely eat living plants, so gardeners should not consider them pests. On the whole they do much more good than harm, and are especially useful in chewing up plant fragments in compost heaps. The woodlouse is not an insect but a crustacean, that has 14 parts to its body, which gives the woodlouse the flexibility to be able to curl into a ball to protect itself from danger. This means that only the hard outer shell of the woodlouse is exposed.

## Slugs

Slugs are familiar slimy pests that cause havoc in the garden, eating and making holes in leaves, stems, flowers, tubers and bulbs. There are about seven species of slug that are garden pests. They can cause damage throughout the year to a wide range of plants, but seedlings and new growth on herbaceous plants in spring are most at risk and may need protection. Slugs remain active throughout the year, unlike snails, which are dormant during autumn and winter. Warmer weather, combined with damp conditions greatly increases their activity. Slugs are most active after dark or in wet weather. Slugs vary in size from the grey field slug (Deroceras reticulatum), which is no more than 5cm (about 2in) long, to the large black slug (Arion ater), which can be 12cm (about 5in) when fully extended. Some slugs vary in colour; the Arion ater can be black, orange-brown or buff coloured.

## Snails

Snails are one of the earliest known types of animal in the world. There is evidence that they evolved more than 600 million years ago. As a snail moves it leaves behind a trail of slime. This allows it to easily move across any type of terrain without injuring its body. They aren't able to hear at all so they rely on their sense of touch to interact with each other. They use their sense of smell to help them find food. Snails range in size from 30cm to 15in in length. Snails don't like the brightness of sunlight which is why you will find them out more on cloudy days. If you keep one in an aquarium you need to make sure that too much sunlight doesn't filter into the room. This can cause the snail to stop eating and to spend most of its time inside its shell.

# Minibeast rhymes and poems

### Firefly
Firefly, firefly,
Come from the hill,
your father and mother
are waiting here still.
They've brought you some sugar,
some candy, and meat,
for baby to eat.

(Traditional Chinese nursery rhyme)

### Here is the beehive
Here is the beehive
but where are the bees?
Hidden away
where nobody sees.
Look and you'll see them
come out of the hive,
One, Two, Three, Four, Five,
Bzzzzzzzzzzzz.

### Hong Ching-Ting (Red Dragonflies)
| | |
|---|---|
| Hong ching-ting. | Red dragonflies |
| Ching ching ting. | Gently stop. |
| Shih shang ching ching ting, | On the rocks gently they stop, |
| Shui shang ching ching ting, | On the water gently they stop, |
| Feng li ching ching ting. | In the breeze gently they stop. |
| (Traditional Chinese nursery rhyme) | (English translation) |

## Incy Wincy Spider

Incy Wincy Spider climbed up the spout.
Down came the rain
and washed the Spider out.
Out came the sunshine,
and dried up all the rain.
Incy Wincy Spider,
climbed up the spout again.

## Ladybird, Ladybird

Ladybird, ladybird,
fly away home.
Your house is on fire,
and your children all gone.
All except one,
and that's Ann,
for she has crept under,
the frying pan.

## The worm

There's a worm at the bottom of my garden
And his name is Wiggly Woo.
There's a worm at the bottom of my garden
And all that he can do...
Is wiggle all night
And wiggle all day.
Whatever else the people do say;
There's a worm at the bottom of my garden
And his name is Wiggly, Wig-Wig-Wiggly,
Wig-Wig-Wiggly Woo-oo!

### The butterfly

How does a butterfly go?
Hey ho does anybody know?
How does a butterfly go?
A flutter, flutter all day long.

How does an earthworm go?
Hey ho does anybody know?
How does an earthworm go?
A wriggle, wriggle all day long.

How does a little cricket go?
Hey ho does anybody know?
How does a little cricket go?
A hopping, hopping all day long.

How does a cockroach go?
Hey ho does anybody know?
How does a cockroach go
A scuttle, scuttle all day long.

# Useful books

## Adult books

The Time-Saving Garden
(Readers Digest 2007)

How to Plant Your Allotment by Caroline Foley
(New Holland Publishers Ltd 2007)

## Children's books

Are you a snail? by Judith Allen and Tudor Humphries
(Kingfisher press, 2000)

Bartholomew and the Bug by Neal Layton
(Hodder childrens books, 2009)

Billy's Beetle by Mick inkpen
(Hodder and Stoughton, 2007)

Bugs and Slugs by Judy Tatchell
(Usborne, 1999)

Centipede (Bug Books) by Chris Macro, Karen Hartley and Phil Taylor
(Heinemann library, 2006)

Ladybird (Bug Books) by Chris Macro and Karen Hartley
(Heinemann Library, 2006)

Snail (Bug Books) by Chris Macro, Karen Hartley, and Jill Bailey
(Heinemann library, 2006)

Minibeasts (themes for early years) by Avril Harpley and Ann Roberts
(Scholastic, 1997)

Snail Trail by Ruth Brown
(Anderson press, 2010)

Ten wriggly wiggly caterpillars by Debbie Tarbet
(Little Tiger Press, 2009)

The Bad-tempered ladybird by Eric Carle
(Puffin, 2010)

The Very Busy Spider by Eric Carle
(Puffin, 1996)

The Very Hungry Caterpillar by Eric Carle
(Puffin, 1995)

The Very Quiet Cricket by Eric Carle
(Puffin, 1997)

## Useful websites

www.buglife.org.uk

www.gardenersworld.com/how-to/projects/category/creative-projects/

www.rspb.org.uk/advice/gardening/insects

http://mylearning.org/interactive.asp?journeyid=77&resourceid=311

http://teachers.ash.org.au/jmresources/minibeasts/minibeasts.htm

www.mis.coventry.ac.uk/·nhunt/180sor/ogrady/Minibeasts.htm

www.tes.co.uk/article.aspx?storyCode=6012200

www.sac.sa.edu.au/Library/Library/Primary/themes/minibeasts.htm

www.childmindinghelp.co.uk/forum/showthread.php?t=31950 (registered childminder's forum)

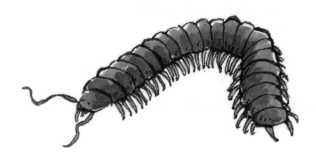

# The Little Books Club

There is always something in Little Books to help and inspire you. Packed full of lovely ideas, Little Books meet the need for exciting and practical activities that are fun to do, address the Early Learning Goals and can be followed in most settings. Everyone is a winner!

We publish 5 new Little Books a year. Little Books Club members receive each of these 5 books as soon as they are published for a reduced price. The subscription cost is £37.50 – a one off payment that buys the 5 new books for £7.50 instead of £8.99 each.

In addition to this, Little Books Club Members receive:
- Free postage and packing on anything ordered from the Featherstone catalogue
- A 15% discount voucher upon joining which can be used to buy any number of books from the Featherstone catalogue
- Members price of £7.50 on any additional Little Book purchased
- A regular, free newsletter dealing with club news, special offers and aspects of Early Years curriculum and practice
- All new Little Books on approval - return in good condition within 30 days and we'll refund the cost to your club account

Call 0207 6315822 or email: littlebooks@bloomsbury.com
for an enrolment pack. Or download an application form from our website:

## www.acblack.com/featherstone